BEHOLD YOUR KING

A FAMILY ADVENT GUIDE

BY GRANT AND ERICHA VAN BRIMMER,
WITH SCOTTY AND SONDRA ROWLETT

Published by EICC Publications,
a ministry of the Ezra Institute for Contemporary Christianity,
PO Box 9, Stn. Main, Grimsby, ON L3M 1M0

By Grant and Ericha Van Brimmer, with Scotty and Sondra Rowlett. Edited by Ben Emery. Copyright of the authors, 2018. All rights reserved. This book may not be reproduced, in whole or in part, without the written permission of the publishers.

Cover art and interior illustrations by Trung Duong, cover design and layout by Kathy Jimenez.

Unless otherwise noted, Scripture quotations are taken from the English Standard Version © 2001 by Crossway Bibles, a division of Good News Publishers. Used by permission.

For volume pricing please contact the Ezra Institute for Contemporary Christianity: info@ezrainstitute.ca.

Behold Your King: A Family Advent Reader

ISBN: 978-1-989169-08-7

Table of Contents

Introduction 5
Daily Meditations 7
Appendix: Christmas Carols 39

INTRODUCTION

For hundreds of years, the Christian church has celebrated the season of Advent. Advent is all about anticipation. In this season we anticipate the arrival of our Messiah, the fulfillment of thousands of years of God's promises. There are many good reasons Christians ought to celebrate Advent. As children of God, and as subjects of our King, who have been redeemed from sin and death by His sacrifice, whose Spirit has given us new hearts in place of our old, stony ones, we enjoy a great and gracious privilege in this season. Holiday celebrations carry deeper, richer meaning for God's people, as we rejoice in the hope of reconciliation, and the fruition of God's promises. These promises took definite shape at the birth of our King, Jesus Christ.

The title of this Advent guide, "Behold Your King," is taken from the classic Christmas hymn *O Holy Night*:

Behold your King, Before Him lowly bend!
Truly He taught us to love one another;
His law is love and His gospel is peace.
Chains shall He break for the slave is our brother;
And in His name, all oppression shall cease.

The tone of this hymn is saturated with hope. And like the hymn, this guide is decidedly optimistic, based on the recognition that Jesus is King indeed. It's because of His Kingship that we invite you to not only rejoice in, but also to share the good news of His coming with the world. These classic Christmas carols give voice to a sure and certain hope, and as faithful subjects of our King, we delight to witness to His Kingship that stretches over all of creation – in the words of another carol, He comes to make His blessings flow as far as the curse is found.

It's easy for the Christmas season to become a hurried and chaotic time. This Advent guide is meant to serve as a kind of pause button, making space for a more purposeful celebration of the birth of King Jesus. From the nativity readings, as well as Old and New Testament readings of expectation and of promises fulfilled, hope-filled Christmas hymns, and daily discussion questions, we pray that this Advent devotional will encourage your family this holiday season to stay anchored in the most important reality.

This guide is for the whole family and is designed to be a help in establishing a tradition and liturgy of celebration of our King's arrival. The readings are divided into five different five-day cycles. Every five days you will read through the nativity story, but in a fresh way each time, in light of other Scripture readings and devotional readings, in order to draw out a variety of truths about Jesus' Kingship and how it affects Christians today. Our hope is that as you become more familiar with these nativity passages, and the hymns based on them, your family will come to a greater appreciation and a deeper understanding of the glorious rule of Jesus, and that you and yours would Behold Your King!

WEEK 1

HYMN
Hark the Herald Angels Sing

SCRIPTURE READING
Genesis 3:15

NARRATIVE READING
Luke 1:26-28

Every Christmas season Christians participate in various advent countdowns. Through this joyous season, we delight in the celebration of our Saviour's birth. However, it's important to remember what we needed saving *from* – the dreadful curse of sin! In Genesis 3:15 we see enmity being placed between Satan's seed and Eve's. Graciously, God promised Eve (and her offspring) that one day an heir would be born who would crush the head of Satan, her great enemy.

The heir promised to Eve is the Son who was conceived in the virgin Mary, by the Holy Spirit, that we read about in Luke's narrative. Jesus was born to save us from the dreadful curse of sin. In contrast to Eve's disobedience, which brought about the curse, Jesus perfectly obeys His Father and receives the dominion and rule over the earth that our first parents lost in the garden. In tomorrow's Scripture reading we learn that God promised dominion and kingly rule to Jacob's son Judah. As Luke tells us, Jesus descended from the line of Judah. BECAUSE OF KING JESUS there will be no end to the house of Jacob, nor of His kingdom's expansion, since He lives and reigns forever.

QUESTIONS

1. *What promise is being made about Jesus in Genesis 3:15?*

2. *When Adam and Eve disobeyed God they lost the right to rule creation. How does Gabriel's promise to Mary bring hope of Christ's rule and reign?*

3. *Luke 1:37 states that "nothing is impossible with God." When we look at this story, what are some "impossibilities" that God overcame?*

HYMN
O Come, O Come Emmanuel

SCRIPTURE READING
Genesis 49:10

NARRATIVE READING
Luke 1:39-56

After a long journey, a pregnant Mary arrives in the home of her cousin Elizabeth, herself also pregnant. After Mary enters the house, Elizabeth and her preborn baby (who we know to be John the Baptist) immediately recognize that the child growing in Mary's womb is their Lord. The baby leaps for joy in the womb and Elizabeth, filled with the Spirit, expresses her joy at their arrival with a profound and insightful statement:

"Who am I that the mother of my Lord should come to me?"

Jesus' rule and Lordship was promised and prophesied long ago. His kingship is even recognized by Elizabeth and her preborn child. The scepter and staff spoken of in Genesis 49:10 are symbolic of the kingly authority given to the tribe of Judah. This kingly status is given to Jesus, Himself a descendant of the tribe of Judah. The tribute promised to King Jesus is the inheritance of His people. Elizabeth and John are among the first of this inheritance as they are filled with the Holy Spirit. BECAUSE OF KING JESUS all those who confess Jesus as Lord, including you and I, are made a part of this inheritance.

QUESTIONS

1. Why did the baby John leap for joy when his mother, Elizabeth, came into the presence of Mary and her preborn Son?

2. In Luke 1:47, Mary calls God her Saviour. In verse 49 she says, "He who is mighty has done great things for me." What mighty thing has God done for Mary and how is He her Saviour?

3. Since the scepter and staff are symbolic of Jesus' eternal authority, how does Mary's prayer contrast Jesus' rule with earthly rulers?

HYMN
O Holy Night

SCRIPTURE READING
Isaiah 9:2-3

NARRATIVE READING
Luke 2:1-20

While the shepherds are out tending to their flocks in the darkness, the angel of the Lord appears to them and says, "fear not!" The fear experienced by the shepherds was a natural response. Not only were they walking in literal darkness, but they were also living in a land that was under a curse of spiritual darkness. They were unfit to behold the glory of God. No one born under the curse of this darkness should expect to see God's glory and live (Exodus 33:20) for God cannot dwell with sin (Psalm 5:4). The world needed a mediator, someone to stand in the gap, so it could behold the glory of God.

When the angel proclaims, "fear not and behold," it is an invitation to know the Great Light (John 8:12). One of the great blessings of Jesus' incarnation is seen in the mercy shown to all those that can behold God's glory and live. BECAUSE OF KING JESUS we no longer have to fear the presence of God; instead we are invited to commune with Him face to face.

QUESTIONS

1. *Why do you think that the shepherds feared the glory of God?*

2. *How did the command from the Angel to "fear not," but "behold," calm their fears?*

3. *Who is called the Light of the world and why?*

DAY 4

HYMN
O Come All Ye Faithful

SCRIPTURE READING
Exodus 13:1-16

NARRATIVE READING
Luke 2:21-38

During Israel's time of slavery in Egypt, God judged Pharaoh by sending the angel of death to kill every firstborn son. Placing the blood of a spotless lamb on the Israelites' doorposts was the requirement for them to be spared from God's wrath. This is the reason why God instructed His people, in the Law, to dedicate their firstborn to the Lord. Firstborn animals were dedicated as sacrifices and firstborn sons were "dedicated to redemption" (Exodus 13:13). By setting apart the firstborn, the people of Israel were reminded of God's saving work through the Passover Lamb's blood. Their firstborns were spared from the wrath of the angel of death.

Therefore, when Jesus was yet an infant, in fulfillment of the Mosaic law, His parents brought Him, their firstborn, to the temple to be dedicated. Unlike any other child, while Mary and Joseph were having Him dedicated, God was also dedicating Him to be the spotless Lamb of God; a sacrifice that would redeem all of God's children. BECAUSE OF KING JESUS we no longer need to splatter blood on our doorposts because we have been permanently washed by His blood that was shed for us on His cross.

QUESTIONS

1. When the Israelites were slaves in Egypt, who was it that freed them from their bondage to Pharaoh?

2. How is Jesus' birth, life and death the ultimate fulfillment of the Israelites' exodus from Egypt?

3. Why was it important for Jesus to follow the laws of God, even needing to be dedicated in the temple?

HYMN
Joy to the World

SCRIPTURE READING
Zechariah 8:7-8

NARRATIVE READING
Matthew 2:1-12

God's grand plan to save a people for Himself has always been a multi-ethnic plan; even calling wise men from the East to worship their Saviour. He draws His people to Himself from all corners of the Earth. He never intended to only save one group of people. The flock of Israel is a diverse arrangement of sheep, all being shepherded by the same Good Shepherd, Jesus. His rule is so encompassing that all kings everywhere must bend their knee to Him. *"All the nations you have made shall come and worship before you, O Lord, and shall glorify your name"* (Psalm 86:9).

The wise men showed that their allegiance was to King Jesus when they departed for their homeland and obeyed the Spirit's prompting, defying Herod's command. Their actions reveal to us that they knew Jesus to be the true King. Though Herod sought to destroy his assumed rival, nothing could stop the plan that God had in store for his Son. BECAUSE OF KING JESUS we are able to exercise the dominion that was lost by Adam in the Garden because all authority has been given to Him. Even Satan, the ruler of darkness, has lost his claim to earthly dominion.

QUESTIONS

1. *Who was Jesus born to redeem?*
2. *Based on their route home, who did the wise men fear more, God or Herod?*
3. *Could anything truly stop God's grand plan of redemption?*

WEEK 2

HYMN
Hark the Herald Angels Sing

SCRIPTURE READING
John 1:1-14

NARRATIVE READING
Luke 1:26-38

In the beginning, Jesus, the Word (Logos) of God formed and molded the creation. The Son was God's chosen agent to bring all of creation into being. Now at His advent, Jesus, the Word made flesh, was the beginning of a new creation. Long ago He had created the sun to separate the light from the darkness. Now the hope of a newer and more glorious morn was growing quietly in the womb of His mother, Mary. The power of the Most High overshadowed Mary, accomplishing what she could not with her creaturely limits, and allowing the light of the world to begin to shine.

All the cursed creation eagerly awaited its long-expected Redeemer. The darkness would not just be relegated to a corner of the world, it would be completely overcome and defeated. BECAUSE OF KING JESUS our creaturely limits are also overcome and redeemed. Our sin nature renders us unable to chase our own darkness away. When King Jesus rules in us, the darkness begins to flee. The Creator of all things is able to create a right spirit in us, provoking us to spread the news of the new life that is only found in Him.

QUESTIONS

1. *Was Jesus involved in the initial creation of the universe? How?*
2. *How did Jesus' human form and nature bring hope to a sin-cursed world?*
3. *How did Jesus' divine nature bring hope to a sin-cursed world?*

HYMN
O Come, O Come Emmanuel

SCRIPTURE READING
Isaiah 7:14

NARRATIVE READING
Matthew 1:18-25

The virgin giving birth to the Saviour had long been prophesied. The specific prophecy in today's reading from Isaiah was made 700 years before Jesus was born! This Son of David born to Mary would one day be heir to an everlasting throne. When the angel instructed Joseph to raise the child that was growing in Mary, he referred to Joseph as a son of David. This reference to David carried significant covenantal and prophetic weight to it. The promises of 2 Samuel 7:12-13 likely flooded into Joseph's memory:

> *When your days are fulfilled and you lie down with your fathers, I will raise up your offspring after you, who shall come from your body, and I will establish his kingdom. He shall build a house for my name, and I will establish the throne of his kingdom forever.*

At last, the Davidic line was receiving its final kingly installation. BECAUSE OF KING JESUS the promises made to King David are fulfilled as there is no end to His rule and reign. His eternal nature as the Son of God means no further heir or king will ever be necessary.

QUESTIONS

1. *What family dynasty was Joseph from?*
2. *How does Jesus fulfill the promise that God made to David?*
3. *How did Joseph respond to the news of Jesus' coming?*

HYMN
O Holy Night

SCRIPTURE READING
Micah 5:1-20

NARRATIVE READING
Luke 2:1-20

"He shall stand and shepherd his flock in the strength of the Lord" (Micah 5:4).

The Ruler born in Bethlehem was a lowly babe, dwelling in an animal barn. He would become the Good Shepherd (John 10:11), and shepherd the flock given to Him by His Father (John 10:29).

When the angels appeared to the local shepherds who were out tending to their flocks, they prompted the shepherds to go worship the true Shepherd. At once, they went to behold their superior, Jesus. The Good Shepherd would one day lay His life down for His sheep, Himself becoming the lamb sacrificed to redeem His people and fulfilling what the prophet Micah had written 500 years earlier.

BECAUSE OF KING JESUS the lost sheep have been gathered into the Father's fold. The lowly babe that was born in Bethlehem did not remain in humility but is now exalted to the right hand of the Father. He has been given all authority to expand His flock and rule His Kingdom forever.

QUESTIONS

1. Why did the angels declare the birth of Jesus to shepherds?
2. How did the shepherds find Jesus?
3. Why is Jesus called the Good Shepherd?

HYMN
O Come All Ye Faithful

SCRIPTURE READING
Isaiah 46:13

NARRATIVE READING
Luke 2:21-38

When Simeon held the Christ, the consolation of Israel, he knew that salvation was at hand. God had not delayed in bringing His promised salvation to the world. For hundreds of years God's people had been waiting for the Messiah, God's promised Deliverer and Saviour. Simeon recognized that the Lord's salvation was now at hand; the Lord had brought His righteousness near.

This salvation was not only for the Jews, but also for the Gentile nations. Simeon says that Jesus was "a light for revelation to the Gentiles." Jesus was born to redeem all the nations of the world. The salvation of Israel was always meant to be a light and witness to the Gentile nations. The darkness that had once loomed over the dispossessed and fallen creation was now chased away by the light of Christ. His birth had brought hope to a cursed world. BECAUSE OF KING JESUS Jews and Gentiles are united as one people, into one kingdom, sharing the same King.

QUESTIONS

1. *What had Simeon been promised in a dream?*
2. *How many nations was Jesus born to save?*
3. *What brought comfort to the aging man, Simeon?*

HYMN
Joy to the World

SCRIPTURE READING
Isaiah 11:1-11

NARRATIVE READING
Matthew 2:1-12

The shoot of Jesse promised in Isaiah had taken root and was residing in Bethlehem. He was sitting on the lap of His mother when the wise men arrived to visit Him. The wise men worshipped Him despite being a little boy, proving that they knew Jesus was the true "King of the Jews." After offering Him their gifts, they returned to their home in the East. The promised "shoot of Jesse" had now taken root in their hearts.

Just as a root system begins small but spreads and winds itself deep into the earth, so too the news of Jesus' coming was beginning to spread, and soon His fame would be brought to all nations of the earth. Soon after Jesus ascended into heaven, the book of Acts tells us that the gospel was already reaching the ends of the known world. BECAUSE OF KING JESUS we are commissioned to continue to spread the Good News of His triumph over His enemies. We are commissioned to cultivate that root system until Jesus comes again.

QUESTIONS

1. *Jesus is referred to as the shoot of whom?*
2. *From where did the wise men travel?*
3. *Where did the wise men go after they visited Jesus?*

DAY 11

HYMN
Hark the Herald Angels Sing

SCRIPTURE READING
Numbers 24:17

NARRATIVE READING
Luke 1:26-28

Numbers 24:17 promises the destruction of Israel's enemies by one brought forth from Jacob. When the angel appeared to Mary, he unfolded and explained God's plan to her. The newly conceived Son would be the one to reign over the house of Jacob forever and bring salvation to God's people by destroying its enemies, fulfilling what Numbers 24:17 had prophesied. Mary's response to the angel was exemplary, "let it be to me according to your word." The Word that would become flesh and dwell among us was the promised ruler from Jacob, the one to crush the head of God's enemies.

The only way for God to truly and finally redeem His people would be through the final defeat of Satan, sin, and death. Since Adam and Eve succumbed to the devil's wiles, darkness held dominion over the earth. BECAUSE OF KING JESUS Satan and sin have been conquered and we look forward in expectation to the day when Jesus places His final enemy, death, under His feet in victory.

QUESTIONS

1. *How long would Mary's Son reign over the house of Jacob?*
2. *How did Mary respond to the news of Jesus?*
3. *What is the last enemy to be placed under Jesus' feet in victory?*

HYMN
O Come, O Come Emmanuel

SCRIPTURE READING
Genesis 15:1-6

NARRATIVE READING
Luke 1:39-56

Abram, who would later become "Father Abraham," received a word from God in a vision. Even though Abram was well advanced in years, God made a covenant with him and with his offspring and promised him and his wife a son. This covenant was for the increase of a nation, one that would come from Abram's own family. God called Himself Abram's shield and reward. Mary understood that the birth of her son was the fulfillment of God's covenant "to Abraham and to his offspring forever."

Jesus' new covenant was established by the breaking of His own body, using it to shield all of Abram's true descendants from the wrath of God. BECAUSE OF KING JESUS we no longer have to fear the wrath that was rightly directed toward us. Instead, we are given the blessing of being part of God's covenant family through the work of Jesus on our behalf.

QUESTIONS

1. *Who made a covenant with Abram?*
2. *Aside from Abram, who else did God make the covenant with?*
3. *How is Jesus' new covenant the fulfillment of the Abrahamic covenant?*

HYMN
O Holy Night

SCRIPTURE READING
2 Samuel 7:12-13

NARRATIVE READING
Luke 2:1-20

When God established His covenant with King David, He had promised David a son that would rule on the throne and promised to establish His kingdom forever. The people of Israel had long waited for a descendant of David to come to rule and bring salvation.

The birth of Jesus in the city of David was a fulfillment of prophecy. The Davidic family, which Joseph was a part of, and which Jesus was born into, was also a promise realized. Jesus is the eternal King and Ruler of David's throne. Jesus built an eternal home in the hearts of His people. The presence of God is not confined to a temple, but now resides within His covenant people.

The history of humanity is filled with people being ruled by sinful, inconsistent and tyrannical kings and rulers. BECAUSE OF KING JESUS we have been brought under perfect leadership and placed in harmonious fellowship with God.

QUESTIONS

1. Who established a covenant with David?
2. Aside from David, who was included in God's covenant with David?
3. How does Jesus build a house for God's name?

HYMN
O Come All Ye Faithful

SCRIPTURE READING
Isaiah 49:6

NARRATIVE READING
Luke 2:21-38

As Simeon held the Light of the nations in his arms, he foretold of the fall of all those who would reject that great Light. The Israelites were judged for rejecting their Messiah, but as the Light of the nations, not just Israel, all those who reject Him will be judged.

By receiving the judgment on behalf of His covenant people, Jesus is able to raise up the tribes of Jacob and bring back the preserved remnant of Israel. He brought unity not only to Israel but to all nations and created peace between man and God. Jesus is now building his kingdom from people of every nation through the preaching of the Gospel.

BECAUSE OF KING JESUS, who was called the Light of the world (John 8:12), what was broken is now restored, what was lost is now found, and what was divided is now united.

QUESTIONS

1. What did Simeon say would happen to those who would reject Jesus?
2. Who would bring the rise and reunion of the nation of Jacob?
3. What title does Jesus claim in John 8:12?

HYMN
Joy to the World

SCRIPTURE READING
Micah 4:1-4

NARRATIVE READING
Matthew 2:1-12

The promise of the nations being drawn from all corners of the earth is a story of redemption that continues to advance through history, even to present day. God's plan through all of time has been to redeem what was lost so long ago. Adam lost dominion over the world to the devil. Since that time, God has been working out His plan of redemption in order to undo sin's devastation.

Herod sought to destroy the establishment of Jesus' kingdom. In an effort to prevent their return home Herod misled the wise men by requesting a report so that he might worship Jesus as well, but God's plan had already been set in motion. Even Herod the Great, the most powerful man in Judea, was impotent to frustrate the plan of God. When God speaks forth a proclamation, nothing and no one can stop its advancement. The sovereignty of God is matchless.

BECAUSE OF KING JESUS no scheme devised against God will prevail. Jesus has perfectly accomplished all that was set forth for Him by the Father.

QUESTIONS

1. *Is it possible to change God's plans?*
2. *How did Herod feel about the newly born "King of the Jews"?*
3. *How can we continue to spread the good news of Jesus' birth?*

WEEK 4

DAY 16

HYMN
Hark the Herald Angels Sing

SCRIPTURE READING
Revelation 5:5-10

NARRATIVE READING
Luke 1:26-38

The fears that Mary initially experienced quickly subsided after hearing Gabriel's promise. The promise of the newborn King and of His great and eternal rule caused her heart to rejoice in song.

Her Son would one day be slain to ransom His people from their sin. He alone is worthy to sit at the right hand of God's throne and rule all the nations. We are not certain of the full extent of Mary's comprehension of this promise; however, we do know that it caused her to have peace in the presence of the angel, and to worship God with this song.

The same response is noted of John and the heavenly creatures mentioned in Revelation. When they witness Jesus' ability to open the sealed scroll, their fears subside, and they begin to sing. BECAUSE OF KING JESUS our hearts are also motivated to worship in song because of the redemption He brings. He instills peace where there was once only fear.

QUESTIONS

1. Why do you think Mary had cause for fear?
2. How does Mary respond to the good news given to her by the angel?
3. Why is it important that we rejoice and worship God in song?

HYMN
O Come, O Come Emmanuel

SCRIPTURE READING
Isaiah 9:6-7

NARRATIVE READING
Luke 1:39-56

Generations of Israelites looked forward to the coming of the promised Messiah. The eternal nature of His reign was greatly anticipated, and a welcome reprieve from the sinful rulers they were used to.

After centuries of oppression under foreign powers, the Jewish people longed for liberation. Many expected the Messiah to come as a conquering King, destroying their earthly enemies. A humble son of a carpenter, born in a manger, didn't seem to fulfill their expectations. However, when Mary sings of the future generations that would receive the Messiah's mercy, she is filled with joy. She is the one holding the long-expected King in her belly, and one day He would hold the government on His shoulders.

After redemption was accomplished and Jesus ascended to the right hand of the Father, He was given all authority to rule every nation. BECAUSE OF KING JESUS we are liberated from our oppressors and brought under His gracious rule. Our true enemies – Satan, sin, and death – are driven back and destroyed.

QUESTIONS

1. *Were all of Israel's kings godly kings?*
2. *What are some of the names given to Jesus in today's Scripture reading?*
3. *The good news of Jesus brought Mary joy. What does she sing about?*

HYMN
O Holy Night

SCRIPTURE READING
John 6:35

NARRATIVE READING
Luke 2:1-20

Throughout Israel's history the tabernacle and temple were the places where God met with His people. At Jesus' birth, that all changed. Now, God Himself took on flesh and dwelt among His people, "tabernacling" with them (John 1:14). Inside the temple was the bread of presence. This bread was eaten by the priests and each week it was replaced with new bread. It symbolized the nearness of God and the nourishment that He provided for His people.

The name of the town Jesus was born in, *Bethlehem*, means "House of Bread." Jesus' birth in the town called "House of Bread" reminds us of the bread of presence. Jesus calls Himself the bread of life (John 6:35), offering much-needed sustenance to His people. BECAUSE OF KING JESUS we no longer need to replace the bread of presence each week, because His presence provides for us eternal nourishment.

QUESTIONS

1. *What does the name Bethlehem mean in Hebrew?*
2. *What did the bread of presence that resided in the temple represent?*
3. *What title is given to Jesus in John 6:35?*

HYMN
O Come, All Ye Faithful

SCRIPTURE READING
Isaiah 61:1-3

NARRATIVE READING
Luke 2:21-38

In Luke 2 we are told the story of Anna, an 84-year-old prophetess, dedicated to worship and prayer at the temple. She was widowed at a young age, and likely lived a life of mourning. The loss of her husband made such an impact that she never remarried.

While Anna was worshipping in the temple, Jesus was brought in to be dedicated. Upon seeing Jesus, Anna began to give thanks to the Lord and rejoiced in the coming of her Redeemer. The year of the Lord's favor that Isaiah prophesied (Is. 61:2) had now begun. This brought comfort to Anna and she was clothed in a garment of praise (Is. 61:3) in contrast to the faint spirit that she was burdened with for so many years. All who meet their Redeemer experience the same exchange.

BECAUSE OF KING JESUS our mourning is also turned into rejoicing and our faint spirits are turned into a garment of praise.

QUESTIONS

1. *Why did Anna the prophetess stay at the temple?*
2. *What brought sorrow to Anna's life?*
3. *When Anna knew of Jesus' birth, how did she respond?*

HYMN
Joy to the World

SCRIPTURE READING
Psalm 2:7-8

NARRATIVE READING
Matthew 2:1-12

The nations are a heritage belonging to Jesus, given to Him by His Father. The wise men's allegiance to Jesus commenced the international redemption of the nations. The fact that the ends of the earth belong to the Christ child means that all those who align themselves to Him should seek to extend the reach of the gospel into the uttermost parts of the earth.

After an encounter with Jesus, the wise men's response was to return to their home and spread the news of Christ's Kingship there. The Great Commission (Matthew 28:19) encourages us to continue the mission of bringing the good news of the gospel to all nations by discipling them.

BECAUSE OF KING JESUS we are given His power and authority as ambassadors of the gospel of reconciliation. The message of reconciliation is that enemies become friends. We who were once His enemies are now His friends and we are tasked with bringing even more of Jesus' enemies into his Kingdom.

QUESTIONS

1. *Who gave Jesus the nations?*
2. *How far should the good news of the gospel spread?*
3. *How can we continue to spread the gospel of Jesus?*

WEEK 5

HYMN
Hark the Herald Angels Sing
SCRIPTURE READING
Mark 10:46-52
NARRATIVE READING
Luke 1:26-35

Jesus' life and ministry were the fulfillment of all the promises made in the Old Testament. Mark's gospel tells the story of the blind beggar, Bartimaeus. Bartimaeus was begging on the street when he heard that "Jesus of Nazareth" was near, and he cried out to the "Son of David." In giving Jesus this title, he is acknowledging that Jesus is the fulfilment of Old Testament prophecy of the coming King.

His first request to Jesus was not to have his sight restored, but rather, for mercy. Bartimaeus knew that his primary need was not physical healing, but spiritual. He needed mercy above all because, like all children born from Adam, Bartimaeus was born into rebellion, a rebellion which all people have participated in, which seeks to overthrow God as king and ruler.

Jesus came to destroy that rebellion and bring His people back into a proper relationship with Himself. In His mercy, King Jesus does not destroy His enemy Bartimaeus, but invites him to join Him in His kingdom.

One day, BECAUSE OF KING JESUS, our physical disabilities will all be healed. The healing of Bartimaeus' eyes is a sneak peak into the removal of sin's curse from all of creation which awaits us in the resurrection.

QUESTIONS

1. *Who was King David?*
2. *Why did Bartimaeus need mercy?*
3. *How did Bartimaeus know that Jesus was able to heal Him?*

HYMN
O Come, O Come Emmanuel

SCRIPTURE READING
Acts 2:1-39

NARRATIVE READING
Luke 1:36-80

In Elizabeth's day, the Holy Spirit had not yet been poured out as it would be on the day of Pentecost; still, the Holy Spirit filled her. Zechariah, Elizabeth's elderly husband, was also filled with the Spirit when he prophesied about Jesus; as well as his own son, John. John grew in the Holy Spirit as he prepared for his upcoming ministry.

While the Holy Spirit was active prior to the ascension of Christ, when King Jesus took His place on the heavenly throne, the Holy Spirit was sent to believers in His fullness. Now He is poured out on believers, enabling a cursed humanity to repent and believe in the High King of heaven.

BECAUSE OF KING JESUS the Holy Spirit is sent to believers as our great Helper. The Spirit stirs our affections, He motivates and empowers us, and aids us in the expansion of Jesus' kingship over all nations.

QUESTIONS

1. *Was the Holy Spirit at work prior to Jesus' ascension to the throne of God?*

2. *What are some of the things that the Holy Spirit does to aid in Jesus' kingdom expansion?*

3. *How can we find comfort in knowing that the Holy Spirit is still at work within us?*

HYMN
O Holy Night

SCRIPTURE READING
Matthew 3:1-17

NARRATIVE READING
Luke 2:1-40

Jesus' name, Immanuel, means "God with us." The incarnation of Jesus was necessary for God's plan of redemption to be fulfilled. Jesus, whom God was so pleased with, garnered this favor by obeying and submitting to His heavenly Father by fulfilling all righteousness. We were all born from Adam, and guilty of the same rebellion that Adam began. However, Jesus gives new birth to all that are His. He graciously gifts the righteousness of Himself, the second Adam, to His people.

BECAUSE OF KING JESUS, we can now be favored by our heavenly Father. The cost of our right standing was great. The Father offered His only begotten son as a substitutionary atonement on the cross to pay the price for sin. Despite the brutality of King Jesus' cross, it brought Him great joy to bestow such a gift upon His people.

QUESTIONS

1. Luke 2:40 and Matthew 3:17 state that God the Father favoured Jesus, why is this so?

2. Why was it important that Jesus was favored by the Father?

3. How was Jesus' obedience triumphant over Adam's sin? *(See also Romans 5:18-19)*

HYMN
O Come, All Ye Faithful

SCRIPTURE READING
Exodus 12:1-14

NARRATIVE READING
Luke 2:41-52

For the Jewish people, the celebration of the Passover feast was an important act of remembrance and obedience. Israel's freedom from Egyptian slavery was miraculous; it also pointed the Jewish people to the greater freedom that would be found in Christ's sacrifice.

The Passover lamb offered protection from God's judgment to the firstborn of all in Egypt. Likewise, Jesus was slaughtered to offer us a reprieve from the judgment we deserve.

Our sin against God has incurred a great debt, causing the angel of death to rightly come our way. Hebrews 9:22 says, "without the shedding of blood there is no forgiveness of sins." Jesus' blood is what covers us and makes atonement for the debt we owed. BECAUSE OF KING JESUS, our Passover Lamb, we can feast at the Lord's table forever, in full communion with God.

QUESTIONS

1. *How is Jesus like the Passover lamb?*

2. *How is Jesus greater than the Passover lamb?*

3. *How has King Jesus, our Passover Lamb, satisfied the angel of death that is rightly seeking the disobedient firstborn of Adam?*

BEHOLD YOUR KING

DAY 25

HYMN
Joy to the World

SCRIPTURE READING
Psalm 110

NARRATIVE READING
Matthew 28:16-20

You may not think of Psalm 110 as ringing with Christmas cheer, but it's interesting to note that these are the ones most frequently quoted verses elsewhere in the Bible Scripture. Many prophets and apostles quote this Psalm. Jesus Himself quotes it during His temptation.

In the past 24 days we have learned about Jesus' birth, life and death, but the story of King Jesus is not complete without the good news prophesied in Psalm 110, the good news of His ascension.

The fact that Jesus is currently at the Father's right hand means He is able to make intercession for us. The psalmist also tells us that from His seat of authority, Jesus is doing something more than just advocating for His people; He is ruling in power.

All authority has been given to Him by the Father. His rule extends to the nations and He has given His subjects the work of kingdom expansion. BECAUSE OF KING JESUS we are given power from the Holy Spirit to take back all that belongs to King Jesus.

No longer do Satan and sin have dominion over the earth. The Light of the world has come and chased away the darkness. He has dwelt with His people and redeemed them from their bondage, making all His enemies His footstool.

As far as the curse is found, Jesus' kingdom rule reaches and restores. This is the good news we celebrate at Christmas, and every day as Christians. We are commanded by Jesus to expand the borders of His Kingdom and to share the good news of His Kingship.

In light of this truth, Christian, Behold your King!

QUESTIONS

1. *What is the most-quoted Scripture in all of the Bible?*

2. *Where does Psalm 110 say Jesus currently is?*

3. *Because all authority had been given to Jesus by the Father, what are we instructed to do?*

CHRISTMAS CAROLS

O Holy Night

The Desire of all nations shall come. Hag. 2:7

JOHN S. DWIGHT

ADOLPHE C. ADAM

www.ingramcontent.com/pod-product-compliance
Lightning Source LLC
Chambersburg PA
CBHW060413080526
44583CB00012B/551